ATTAINING THE UNATTAINABLE

Attaining
the
Unattainable

The Will of God

Jim Rosemergy

DeVorss Publications
Camarillo, California

ISBN: 9780875168302
Library of Congress Control Number: 2007920407
First Printing, 2008

DeVorss & Company, Publisher
P.O. Box 1389
Camarillo CA 93011-1389
www.devorss.com

Printed in the United States of America

TABLE OF CONTENTS

God Willin'

"…God willing …if it be God's will." How many people have described some preferred outcome in their lives then added, "if it be God's will"? We usually hope God's will is out-pictured in our personal lives. We wonder if it is God's will that a certain event occur. Is it God's will that we marry our high school sweetheart? Is it God's will that we get the promotion? Is it God's will that we win the contest or that our country triumph in war? Will we be healed? Is it the will of the One that we prosper? Nearly every aspect of human life has been plumbed against the will of God with the hope that God's divine plan is aligned to our desires. Jesus cried out, "…not my will, but yours be done" (Lk. 22:42). Our plea is similar, but profoundly different in its underlying meaning. We wonder if what we want is what God wants for us.

For some people, God's will is violence. Terrorists, captured on video, praised Allah after the Twin Towers in New York fell and the Pentagon was struck. The biblical record of the Hebrews' conquest of Canaan seems to indicate that it was God's will that every man, woman, and child of the city of Ai be utterly destroyed. Christians who conceived the Inquisitions and the Crusades thought they knew the divine will. Many people may find it difficult to believe that God's will is violent, but to question this premise is to question the Bible or at least a literal interpretation of the Scriptures.

So-called "acts of God" are considered expressions of divine will. Insurance companies will insure us against nearly every kind of loss except the ones they say are "acts of God." Somewhere in the policy manuals of the insurance institutions of the world, there is a list of events they believe to be God's will. I wonder if they also believe God's will is joy, oneness, and thankfulness.

Hardly a war has been fought where one side did not evoke the will of the Creator or at least hope that their victory was God's will. The crusaders marched into battle with the image of the cross on their shields. The old hymn, "Onward Christian Soldiers" blends through music and song Christianity and holy battle. Naturally, we believe that to have God on our side is to be assured of victory. During the Civil War, President Lincoln clarified the issue of war and the will of God by saying that his hope was not that God was on the North's side, but that the Union was on God's side. Surely, the will of our loving God draws no line in the sand, but calls us to stand in a circle in which all are equal in the eyes of the One who created us.

As we shall see, the truth is that God's will is not violent and that God draws no lines between nations and tribes. God's view of the world is not a line that divides, but a circle in which the human family is joined in peace and in love's embrace, not locked in conflict.

We are going to explore the will of God. We begin with a look at personal will. We will see it as a coin. One side of this coin leads to willfulness. The other side of the coin is willingness. Some say our will is to be broken. Others advise that it must be surrendered. Still others declare our will must be illumined. We shall see.

In 1986, during a personal retreat, I had an experience that forever changed my view of God's will. Like most people, I plumbed God's will against the events of my life. After the 1986 revelation, the complexity of the divine will fell away, and in its place were two words: "Know Me." We will explore the ramifications of this simple understanding of the will of God. We will find it relevant to our daily lives, and we will discover that the will of God perpetually calls us to action. Rather than wonder if a particular happening is destined to be a part of our life experience, we will hear the call to live a life of joy, thankfulness, and oneness with all life.

For many years, the 1986 experience and its harvest of insights and daily application fed my soul, but then I discovered another dimension of the will of God. It, too, is a call to action. It is not so much that God's will is something

God Willin'

that may or may not happen; it is a way of life. This new understanding of God's will may take your breath away. It did mine. It gave purpose to my life, but it also left me wondering if God's will is attainable. It seemed impossible that such a life could be our destiny, but then again if it is God's will, it must be. And so, dear friend, we move forward together, discovering how to attain the unattainable—the will of God.

CHAPTER 1

Personal Will

It was Jesus who confirmed the obvious: We each have a personal will. "...not my will, but yours be done" (Lk. 22:42). The truth is that we possess more than personal will. We have a will faculty. It is a unique gift from God, for our will can bless us or it can lead us down a path of destruction.

Some religious leaders insist that our will is evil, but it is our will that can keep us alive in the most harsh and dire conditions. I learned this during my training to become a naval aviator. In a survival situation, I could lose many things and survive, but it was paramount that I not lose the will to live. Likewise, prisoners of war in prolonged captivity crack under the duress of ongoing torture only to rise up again as they assert their will once more. We shall find that the will is not to be broken; it is to be illumined. More on this later.

I believe that willingness is the beginning of every successful endeavor. We may not know what to do or even how to begin, but the good news is that the first step is never taken from the outer or physical world. The first step is willingness, and it begins within us. For instance, if we are not well, we must first be willing to be healed. We would think that all people are so inclined, but this is not true. Being healed often means going back to work. It means no longer receiving the sympathy of others. It seems obvious that all people are willing to prosper, but this is not true. When we are filled with guilt, we do not allow ourselves to succeed. We are unwilling to prosper. We think guilty people do not deserve the good life; they don't deserve happiness.

I recall speaking about this with a woman whose life was in chaos. Cheryl knew she had to begin again, but was unwilling to do so. She wouldn't take the next step. The actions required to bring order to her life required courage and a risk of failure. The good news is that her first step was willingness.

Because the world frightened her, I suggested that she begin with willingness. Cheryl spent some time each day gently holding to the statements, "I am willing to begin again. Willingness is my beginning. It is my first step." She verbalized her willingness in the privacy of her home and grew in strength until she could begin to take the tangible steps in the world that would change her life.

Willingness is our beginning. In the days to come, let us be willing to love, willing to feel, willing to be honest with ourselves, and willing to truly live. Willingness may seem like a meager beginning, but with willingness comes energy.

Have you ever established a goal of regular exercise, perhaps four times each week? You had good intentions, but after work you were just too tired to drive to the gym. This is a call for the will faculty and the repeated experience of knowing that, once you get to the gym, you will leave feeling invigorated. Your will is strengthened, and the stronger it becomes, the more you accomplish.

Willingness prepares the way. There have been times in my life when I did not know how to proceed. My first step was to verbally and mentally declare my willingness. Not only would I declare, "I am willing to exercise, forgive, prosper, etc.," but there where times when I identified with willingness and immersed myself in it by using this statement, "I am willingness." In this way, I called into action my faculty of will and opened myself to guidance.

Declaring our willingness is a good beginning, but there comes a time when we must move from the mental realm into the world of action. Finally, we assert our personal will. Athletes do this when they are exhausted, when the fighter returns to the center of the ring or the runner continues to place one foot in front of another even though he or she has hit the wall all marathon runners know lies around the twenty-mile mark. When we assert our will, we act. Persistence keeps us going, but will ignites our fire.

Personal Will

Consider something that you believe you should be doing, but which you are not. This is an opportunity to strengthen your will faculty by putting it to good use. Every time you assert your will, you begin, things are accomplished, and there is the added gift that your will is strengthened.

A strong will is an important part of human life and the spiritual journey, but there is also a paradox. We spend much of our lives strengthening our will only to be asked to surrender it. While Jesus was experiencing one of His passions in the Garden of Gethsemane, He expressed His desire that this "cup" (the trials and crucifixion) be taken from Him, but then He released His will to the will of His Father. It is the surrendering of our will after it has been strengthened that is so difficult for us.

When our will is weak and we accomplish little, there is little to release, but when our will is strong, we tend to think we know best. An unparalleled challenge occurs when we believe our will is God's will. We surge ahead supposedly under divine authority, but no divine plan is unfolding. The result is confusion and chaos. For instance, many terrorists and fanatics believe their murderous actions are the will of God.

The will faculty is a gift from God, but it comes with responsibility. Like all things Spirit gives to us, we tend to believe they are given to enhance our lives, and often they do, but this is not their sole purpose. The day must come when our will is returned to God. It is this surrender that brings triumph. So, dear friend, let us activate our personal will. Let willingness be the beginning of everything we do and even the difficult things will be accomplished. Learn that energy comes when the will is asserted. Each time it is asserted, it grows in strength, but the day will come when our will is illumined. On that day, it is surrendered to God, and we are one step closer to attaining the unattainable.

Remember, the personal will is part of the divine plan. Through it, energy is gathered to us and flows through us. Through personal will, things get done. Some of the things accomplished are a blessing, others are a curse. Each accomplishment strengthens the will and brings us one day closer to the time when we relinquish it and return it to the One who gave us this treasure. On this day, the will of God is made manifest. What seems unattainable today becomes a living reality.

CHAPTER 2

"Know Me"

There is more than one way to describe God's will. On the pages to follow, we will explore various ways of expressing the divine intent in our lives. None will be more correct than another, but my hope is that understanding God's will one way and then another will allow us to experience the fullness of what has mystified humanity for ages. We begin with a mystical experience that changed my life and my understanding of the will of God.

I love to write, and for many years I have explored God, myself, and truth through the written word. I wrote regularly, but usually for only a few nights each week. I wondered if I could write all day for several days.

In 1986, a friend lent me his log cabin so I could conduct my experiment. I arrived on an autumn day and got a fire going in the fireplace, and then placed my Kaypro computer on a card table before the cabin's picture window. I had longed for this creative time for years, and finally it was here. I began to write. I wrote two paragraphs, and suddenly the computer locked up. The cursor would not move. I hit numerous keys and did what all computer people do: I hit the same key over and over again expecting a different result. I changed discs in the computer (this was before the era of internal hard drives), but the cursor continued to blink in its now familiar place. I liked what I had written, so I copied the paragraphs long hand, shut off the computer, and then brought it back on line.

Still the cursor blinked at me. I then realized why they call it a cursor! At this point, I began to lose my sense of the indwelling Presence. I looked up and wondered why this was happening. I pointed out to God that it was Spirit's guidance that had brought me to this place. I had felt the urge to write for an extended period of time, and now, finally, the dream was coming true, or was it? The computer was locked up. It was at this time that I heard a distinct inner voice say to me, "Your purpose is not to write; it is to know Me." Stunned, I returned to the keyboard and hit several keys. The cursor moved, and I wrote for three days. It is interesting that nothing I wrote during this time was published, but the experience of the blinking cursor and the two words, "Know Me," changed my life.

Those two words startled me, but I now know that their simplicity encompasses the expansive will of God. The divine will is not a certain happening. God is beyond all events. The kingdom is not of this world, nor is God's will. It is not selective; it is the same for everyone.

I am married to a wonderful woman and our lives are a joy, but it is not God's will that we are married. The divine will is that Nancy and I know God as love. This constantly unfolding consciousness manifests itself as our marriage and ever deepening relationship. The spiritual union of two individuals is not God's will; ideally the union is the result of each person knowing God as love.

I do not believe it is the will of God that I live and work in a particular place. God is omnipresent, everywhere equally present. However, it is the divine intent that I know God to be with me wherever I am.

This realization tends to demystify God's will and simplifies life. I seek to fulfill Spirit's will -"Know Me." As this consciousness is experienced, it manifests itself in ways that are perfect for this moment in my spiritual journey and earthly life. I am married to Nancy, and I live and work in a specific place such as Fort Myers, Florida.

As you seek to know God as wisdom and as your source, perhaps the company merger you have worked for may occur, or your advertising strategy is approved and another client is added to the roster of your company, but such things are not God's will. Spirit's will is that you know God as wisdom, and creativity flows from this experience. The result is you discover innovative ways for two companies to better serve their markets and clients.

Our lives are to flow from our spiritual lives. They are to flow from an experience of the divine. As we answer the call "Know Me," the mystical experience of God's will becomes practical. This is the balance of earthly life and spirituality. This is God's will transforming and blessing our daily lives.

The King and the Court

Images are sometimes helpful in understanding spiritual insights, so let us assume I am one of a king's ministers of state. I carry out his majesty's edicts and desires. I am knowledgeable in the ways of state, therefore I do not rush into the king's presence and ask him what to do. Nor do I have the audacity to ask the sovereign to serve me or to fulfill my desires. My purpose is to serve the king. I am aware that, first and foremost, the divine intent is that I be in the king's presence.

In this analogy, God is the king and His will is that I dwell consciously in His Presence. Of course, the omnipresent God I serve is always closer than hands and feet, but I am not always aware of the Presence in which I live and move and have my being. Therefore, my purpose is to draw near to the king, to become consciously aware of Spirit. I believe this is God's will.

For too long, I have stood outside the court and shouted my wants and ambitions to the king. I have pleaded in an attempt to have Spirit serve me. The focus was not God's will; instead I yearned to know if God would act on my behalf. Now I can hear Spirit's answer to my pleading, my prayers, and my desires: "Draw consciously close to Me and come to know Me, and then you will know how to live."

Another Analogy

God is at home, and I call to ask if I can come over to visit. Spirit thinks, "Finally, a relationship is going to develop between us." I knock on the door. It opens and I stand before God with an empty container and a question: "Can I borrow a cup of sugar?"

I have not come to know my God (experience God's presence) and to develop a relationship. I need to borrow a cup of sugar. I desire to draw near to God not because I want to call God friend as did Abraham, but because I have a need in my life.

This simple example illustrates the way most of humanity approaches the Creator. We either don't want a relationship or don't realize a relationship is possible; we want an earthly need fulfilled, and typically we wonder if the fulfillment of the need is God's will.

A New Way of Life

There is a way of life that begins with the understanding that God's will is "Know Me." For instance, consider that you have a healing need. In the past, you would assume that God's will is that your body be healed. You ask to be healed and affirm and give thanks that your health is restored. Once again you stand at the door with the cup in your hand. You are asking for something for yourself and ignoring the potential of knowing God.

When you understand that God's will is "Know Me," your approach to life and healing is different. You ask for nothing. You do not say, "God, will you heal me?" Your purpose is to be in the presence of the king. It is to know God. Your soul thirsts for Spirit. Your eye is single and focused on living a spiritual life. As you are prayerful and still, a realization comes...*I am made in the image and after the likeness of God. God is life, and I am divine life being lived. I lack nothing. I am whole.* These truths are revealed from within. You are healed, but something greater than healing occurs. The prodigal has returned, and a friendship is formed. An eternal relationship is remembered. Spirit declares, "All that is mine is yours. All that I am, you are."

We no longer need to ask God for anything or to inquire about a specific event. We know that no event is God's will; the divine will is everlasting and is the same for everyone. As people wonder, "What is God's will?" in the silence of their souls, Spirit declares Its will: "Don't you want to know Me?"

CHAPTER 3

A Way of Life

Beliefs about God's will abound. The Bible reveals that many people believed that everything that happened was God's will. If there was an abundant harvest, the Creator was to be praised. When the crops failed, this, too, was God's work. A triumph in war was God's blessing upon one nation and God's admonition to another to amend its ways.

In the world today, when we consider the Holocaust or the attack on America on September 11, 2001, it is difficult to fathom how anyone could interpret such violent and inhumane acts as the will of God. Using God's will to justify such acts cannot be the will of a loving God. Such beliefs are impossible to reconcile with a God of love.

I believe that the divine intent is not seen in earthly events and the happenings of our lives. I believe the divine will is a particular way of life. In the last chapter, the implications of God's will, "Know Me," were explored. These two words call us to a way of life. They make known the truth that we can have a powerful, meaningful experience and even a relationship with our Creator. Like prodigals wandering in the far country, we can return to the safe haven of a life of oneness with God.

A Way of Life

As outlined in the previous chapter, the two words "Know Me," call us to a way of life where God is at the center. If we have a decision to make, we do not ask God what we should do. Instead, we are willing to experience the Presence as wisdom. From this experience, we discover what we are to do, but much more has transpired than a choice made. We have drawn closer to the One who is light, and this light has shined from within us into our every-day life. Decisions come and go. They command our attention for a time, but are usually forgotten. An experience of the Presence is never forgotten, for it becomes the foundation of an ever-growing relationship with God.

You see, when we have a decision to make, there are greater possibilities before us than simply making a decision. We have the opportunity to become aware of God as light and wisdom. We can become aware that the mind of God dwells in us. This is why I say there is more at stake than a choice to make. The real question is this: Will we open ourselves to a deeper relationship with Spirit, or will we allow this opportunity to pass?

The mystical experience I had many years ago pointed me to a new way of life and to a new relationship with my Creator. I was called to listen and to give attention to something besides my own will and wants and desires. Now whenever I face a challenge, I know that the answer is to know and experience the presence of God. If I falter and want to quit some task, I know that if I know God as strength, I can rise up and begin again. If I am anxious, I know serenity comes when I know God as peace. There is no challenge in life that cannot be met when I know God. This way of life, I believe, is God's will, but I have found this understanding is only the beginning.

Not long ago, I discovered another expression of God's will: "Rejoice always, pray constantly, give thanks in all circumstances; for this is the will of God... "(I Thessalonians 5:16-18). It is obvious that these verses call us to a way of life, but there is one problem: They seem unattainable. How can someone rejoice always? How can we pray constantly or give thanks in all circumstances? Are we being called to do the impossible? Or perhaps it is enough to try. This possibility does not appeal to me. It sows the seeds of frustration. I try, but what I pursue lies just beyond my grasp. Who would begin such a journey?

Here is another consideration: Perhaps there is a way of attaining the unattainable. Surely, this would be the greatest quest. It could change everything. One thing is sure, if the way of life outlined in I Thessalonians is possible, it would lead to a new kind of life for the human family. God's will would no longer be about the world; it would be about our spiritual lives. God's will as

A Way of Life

specific events would forever be put aside, and in their place would be a way of life filled with joy, prayer, and thanksgiving.

We do not yet know the answer as to whether we can actually rejoice always, pray constantly, and give thanks in all circumstances, but this is our next area of investigation. We are moving beyond wondering if some specific happening is God's will. We are putting aside the belief that the Creator is the author of all events and venturing into a new territory called our spiritual lives. The promise is great: perpetual joy and prayer, as well as continuous thanksgiving. Promises, promises, we ponder. Surely, this is impossible, or is it? We shall see. One thing is for certain, the promise is worth our attention, for it holds out to us a life filled with unspeakable happiness.

CHAPTER 4

Rejoice Always

Rejoice always...for this is the will of God...

I Thessalonians 5:16, 18

When Paul wrote his letter to the Thessalonians, I wonder if he realized the high standard he established: *Rejoice always*. Surely this is impossible, unattainable, and yet he calls this way of life the will of God. Perhaps, just perhaps, he is alerting us to our potential, to the way of life we can live.

Here is a foundational principle of *Attaining the Unattainable*: God's will is a way of life. It calls us to action. In this instance, God's will is a life of joy. Rather than wonder whether a certain event is part of the divine plan, we can wonder how we can rejoice always.

I am willing to entertain the possibility that I can rejoice always and live in perpetual joy. If it is God's will, there must be an underlying force that makes possible a life of joy. Such a life is not abnormal; it is attainable. In truth, it is normal.

Jesus' message was one of joy. "These things I have spoken to you, that my joy may be in you, and that your joy may be full" (John 15:11). The joy Jesus felt, we are destined to feel. In this promise, I can see the hand of God and human hands intertwined. We rejoice; we are happy for a time, and then our happiness fades. We lose our joy. We wonder where it went and how we can become reacquainted with that which is so precious. Paul knew this was the human experience. The call is for us to return again and again to joy. We are to know that joy is our destiny. God's will is for us to live lives of joy, not pain and anguish.

We are to search for joy again and again. Joy may fade, but we are not to despair. The delight we once experienced, we can experience again. In fact, we are never to settle for anything less than joy. The prefix "re" means again. This is Paul's message and God's message to us: We are to return again and again to joy. We are to open ourselves to ecstasy. Currently, joy may not be our experience, but it is our destiny.

The human condition may be one in which joy ebbs and flows like the tides, but the driving force of the Universe is that we be happy. Intuitively, most of us know this is true, or we would not consistently pursue joy. Remember, in America happiness is considered the right of all its citizens. This is surely a reflection of the divine will expressing itself in the founding document of a nation.

During a time of prayer and meditation, have you ever experienced a giddiness, a fullness of heart, or an overflowing of happiness and joy? No outer circumstance caused this experience. There is you and there is God, and then suddenly there is only God. And there is joy.

This is what we are looking for, what we are promised: a joy not born of circumstance, but from an experience of the Presence. Sometimes we experience this joy in times of prayer and meditation. At other times, it comes to us when we lose all sense of time. We are fully engaged in some activity, and we enter a state of consciousness called now. In this moment, there is joy. This often happens to me when I write. It is a delight, but since my usual writing time is at night, I find it difficult to get to sleep-so invigorating is the joy!

One of my favorite movies is *Chariots of Fire*. It is a story set in 1924 as two British Olympians, Harold Abrahams and Eric Liddell, both sprinters, pursue the same gold medal. Eric Liddell is a unique man, a man of deep Christian faith. He is destined to be a missionary. In fact, his sister, Jennie, wants him to forego the Olympic games and begin God's work with her in China. In a poignant scene in the movie, Eric tells his sister why he must run in the games.

Rejoice Always

He says that God has made him fast, and to not run would be to dishonor God. To run and win would be to honor the Creator. He tells Jennie that when he runs, he can feel God's pleasure. I never forgot that line: "When I run, I feel His pleasure."

The phrase brought me back to an earlier time in the movie when Eric was running in a race. At first, he ran like any other man, but suddenly his head went back and glee appeared on his face. He seemed to be in an altered state of consciousness out of which he ran faster than the other runners. It was when Eric Liddell felt God's pleasure. This is the height of human experience—to feel God's pleasure. This is what awaits us, and we are never to settle for anything less. If it can happen to a runner during a race, it can happen to us while we are in the midst of life. By using our natural talents for God's purpose and God's glory rather than our own, we experience a joy that transcends the world.

Here is the pattern most, if not all, of us follow. We experience joy and then lose it, but search again. Here we have a promise of a joy that does not come and go. It does not depend upon other people or upon certain happenings. Either in a time of divine friendship in prayer and meditation when we give full attention to the moment, or when we are immersed in expressing our God-given talent, we experience elation.

Recently, I experienced boundless joy. My friend Carl was suffering from a kidney disease and needed a kidney transplant. After much testing, it was determined that my kidney was a match, and the operation was successfully completed. Just the thought of giving my kidney to help Carl live a full life granted me the gift of euphoria. For days, I was in a state of delight so great that I could not contain it. My wife, Nancy, said to me, "Do you know how you are acting?" I said, "Yes, but I can't help it. I am so filled with joy." You see, dear friend, giving is another way in which we experience sheer joy. A life of sharing and giving grants us the full joy that Jesus promised. Joy is God's will and so is giving.

Giving is a path to joy, and it does not matter what you give, only that you do give. As you can imagine, giving one of your organs to another person is serious business. However, I have learned that a person can experience an ecstasy so great that it leaves him or her physically trembling when the gift is a mere dollar bill.

One year, my family and I were vacationing at the beach. Rainy weather did not permit outside play, so we went to a shopping mall to browse the many stores. I was in the sporting goods section of a department store when I saw a boy buying a soccer ball. It was obvious that he did not have enough money to complete the purchase. He was taking money from every pocket in his pants, but he was short less than a dollar. I took a dollar from my wallet and gave it to the clerk to complete the transaction. As soon as the dollar bill left my hand, I felt a bliss so great that I was trembling. It was euphoric just as it was when I was trying to help my friend through a kidney transplant. As I reflected back upon this event in my past, it touched me that the feeling was the same even though the gift was totally different. Obviously, it is the not the nature of the gift that is important; it is that the gift be given freely, and when it is freely given, we will bear as much joy as our frail physical frames will allow!

I once heard a man tell a story about the most profound moment of his life. He was alone and a butterfly landed on him and tarried with him for a time. He said he felt a great oneness with this winged creature and all creation. His joy was full because he gave attention to a butterfly. How often do we fail to see such creatures as they flutter from thing to thing and meander from flower to flower? We might brush this insect away rather than realize that a few moments spent with the butterfly can bring us elation we will never forget.

My sense is that there was a moment of awakening when this man, who was preoccupied in his own thoughts, realized a connection with the butterfly.

Then suddenly, there was more than just a man and a butterfly; there was all creation. In essence, there is only God, and where there is only God, there is pure joy.

It is this way of life God has ordained for us. We are called to return again and again to joy: *Rejoice always.*

Dear friend, don't you dare settle for anything less, for joy is God's will and, therefore, it is your destiny.

CHAPTER 5

Pray Constantly

Pray constantly...for this is the will of God...

I Thessalonians 5:17, 18

It seems inconceivable that anyone could pray constantly. And besides, isn't prayer for times of difficulty? Why would anyone want to perpetually pray?

The good news is that there are those for whom prayer is more than an attempt to have God help them out of their difficulties. For these spiritual seekers, prayer becomes life. They have answered the call to pray constantly, and in their attempt to fulfill the will of God, they discovered life as it is meant to be. Prayer is no longer an attempt to spur the Almighty to action. Prayer is experienced as a state of oneness with the One. This state of mind and heart does not suddenly form because someone prayed; oneness was revealed to be our natural state of being. In fact, it is our perpetual state of being. Oneness does not come into being. It is the truth of our relationship with God now, and prayer is one of the ways through which oneness is discovered.

Pray Constantly

The truth is that God's will is oneness, and it calls us to action. We are to pray, to seek this state of oneness with our Creator. You see, we are one with God, but when we are conscious of our oneness with Spirit, we become avenues of God's power and love. This has always been our destiny, our reason for being. We are a door through which the Creator can create. It is no wonder that God's will is oneness and unity. It is only through a consciousness unified with our Creator that the divine plan of good can be established. And so, we are called to pray constantly, for in this way the divine plan can constantly manifest itself.

Continuous prayer is our greatest challenge; at least it has been for me, but there are those who have lived this way. During the 17th century, Nicholas Herman, who became the Carmelite monk Brother Lawrence, practiced the presence of God. He worked in a monastery hospital kitchen in the mid 1600s and hated it, but then he began an experiment. He wondered if he could live as if there was only he and God. This way of life transformed him until he wrote that he experienced "joys so continual and so great that I can scarce contain them." His daily life, his normal mundane tasks, and his spiritual life were joined. His formal times of prayer were no different from his work. He knew God to be perpetually with him.

This is true for all of us. This is the life we are called to live—conscious oneness with God. Because Brother Lawrence lived this way, people learned of this kitchen helper with the personal relationship with Spirit. Church and secular leaders as well as ordinary people came to him for guidance, and he wrote letters of support to those who wrote to him. Brother Lawrence brought God into every task, and every task became a joyful time with God.

Frank Laubach did the same thing. Laubach wrote over fifty books, but perhaps his most significant work was his journal of his experiment conducted at Signal Hill in the Philippines. Frank Laubach began with a question: Could he bring to mind a thought of God at least once every waking hour? Once this was achieved, he then asked if it was possible to hold in mind an awareness of the Presence each waking minute of his life. It was a grand quest like Brother Lawrence's attempt to practice the Presence, and just as the simple Carmelite monk was transformed, so too was Laubach. Below are some excerpts from his journal as he sought to live in continuous oneness with God.

> January 29, 1930. *This sense of cooperation with God in the little things is what so astonishes me, for I never have felt it this way before.*

March 1, 1930. *The sense of being led by an unseen hand which takes mine while another hand reaches ahead and prepares the way grows upon me daily.*

March 23, 1930. *One question now to be put to the test is this: Can we have contact with God all the time? All the time awake, fall asleep in His arms, and awaken in His presence?*

May 24, 1930. *This concentration upon God is strenuous, but everything else has ceased to be so.*

June 1, 1930. *The most important discovery of my whole life is that one can take a little rough cabin and transform it into a palace just by flooding it with God.*

From Frank Laubach's 20th-century quest to live a life of oneness with God, we turn to an unnamed Russian pilgrim who prayed the prayer of the heart. This practice enabled him to live according to God's will. The pilgrim prayed a "prayer" that may be foreign to many of us, but it became the center of his willingness to pray constantly. At first, he mentally affirmed the following words thousands of times during the day: "Lord Jesus Christ have mercy on me." Often he could be seen with lips moving as he said the prayer again and again. Next, he attempted to wed the prayer to his breathing. As he inhaled, he mentally recited, "Lord Jesus Christ," and then when he exhaled he filled his mind with "have mercy on me." He hoped that eventually, the prayer would pray itself. As he breathed, the words of the prayer would fill his mind. And then he took a step further. He also wed the prayer not only to his breathing, but to his heartbeat. He began by seeing his heart in his chest through the use of his imagination. Once he achieved this image, he recited a word of the prayer with each beat of his heart. As he lived, he prayed, and he lived in oneness with God, thus fulfilling God's will. Every breath declared the prayer. Every heartbeat sent it forth into the world.

If you read *The Way of a Pilgrim*, the book that records the pilgrim's adventures, you will discover that he became an instrument for God's wisdom and love. Because he lived in oneness with God, he became a wick of the candle and an avenue for God's light, word, and work.

I have strived to pray constantly. In other words, I have tried to live a life of conscious oneness with God. The results have been mixed, but it remains the central quest of my life. I believe a life of oneness is the destiny of every human being, and I know that when we live in conscious oneness with God, not only do we experience peace, love, and joy, but we are also avenues for all that we experience. This is the promise. Please do not consider it unattainable; it is the will of God.

We are called to be monks of the city. Most of us have jobs that keep us busy throughout the day. Life calls to us from many quarters, and often we are tossed to and fro by the requests of other people and the demands we place upon ourselves. The great challenge is to find balance, and balance, I have found, comes when I make God a priority.

If we are to practice the Presence, we must persist. We will fail from time to time, but there is no lasting failure unless we fail to rise after we have fallen. Persistence, we will find, is a great ally, but equally so is the power of love.

As we strive to pray constantly, love takes the form of self-acceptance. This is particularly true when we lose our sense of the Presence—and we will lose our awareness of the One. When this happens, we accept ourselves as we are and persist. We begin again. Undoubtedly, the day will come when we begin again and never lose an awareness of our Creator. This momentous day may lie in the future, but it is before us. Let us never doubt that God's will can be experienced.

A foundation principle of a life of oneness with God is the truth that we "live and move and have our being in God." As I was writing this chapter, a thought occurred to me. For years, I have practiced the Presence. I used the practices and techniques of other people such as Frank Laubach, Brother Lawrence, and the Russian pilgrim. These were helpful pursuits, but why didn't I open myself to finding the way I am to fulfill God's will by praying without ceasing?

In a time of prayer and meditation two ideas came to me. The first was to consider that God is watching me in everything that I say and do. For instance, when I speak to a friend or someone is asking for spiritual help, I become aware of God as the Watcher, observing what I say and do. Secondly, the Creator became not an observer, but a full participant in my life. If I am splitting wood, God is splitting wood as well, and God is the wood that is split as well as the steel that penetrates the log. The strength I feel is not my own. In this way, the simplest act reveals the omnipresence of God. God was and is all.

In everything in my life, I can think of God either observing or participating. This practice became special to me for two reasons. The first was that it worked. The second reason was that it came through my consciousness and therefore was something that I needed. It was my practice.

Pray Constantly

There is a legend about a group of highly creative people. In all areas of life they excelled. Generation after generation created masterpieces of literature, art, sculpture, and music. A study was conducted to determine why a group of people could be so productive. Was it a gene or "something in the water"? The researchers found that there was one common ingredient that all the people shared: a story. When the children were seven years old, they were told that the Great Spirit was always with them and could be seen if the children turned quickly and looked over their left shoulders. There was no record of the Great Spirit ever being seen, but there was one common belief: the nearness of God. It was concluded that this made all the difference.

It is obvious that praying without ceasing requires that we acquire the gift of attention. It must become steadfast and consistent. It is to have the single eye and to serve one master, God.

In the spiritual practice and Forty-Day Guide portion of this book, you will find exercises and techniques to try as you strive to pray constantly. They will get you started, and some of them may sustain you for years. But don't hesitate to open yourself to a more personal way of practicing the Presence. Remember, a life of oneness is the true issue, and the Universe will support you in this grand quest.

CHAPTER 6

Give Thanks in All Circumstances

Give thanks in all circumstances...for this is the will of God...

I THESSALONIANS 5:18

We are discovering that God's will is not a thing; it is not a happening. It is life as it is meant to be. God's will is a way of life. Whether it be the call to live a life of joy by rejoicing always or a life of oneness with God and all creation through constant prayer, a high standard is held out to us—one that seems impossible. But our Creator does not tantalize us with unreachable goals and false promises. Our God is truth, and God's truths are the promises upon which our lives are founded.

We now know two of the promises: a life of joy and a life of oneness. Only one more pillar must be added to establish a balanced life that is ordained by God. We are called to give thanks *in* all circumstances. We are called to live a life of thankfulness.

Thanksgiving is a part of most of our lives. Sometimes it is simple courtesy. At other times, it literally opens the windows of heaven. Thanksgiving that is courtesy comes after we receive some blessing, so we give thanks. The gratitude that becomes a doorway to the kingdom of God doesn't require a blessing. It is a choice we make. We choose to be thankful regardless of the situation. In fact, as we shall see, the experience of God's power and presence is often more real because there is no outer thing for which to give thanks.

Unhappy people seldom express heartfelt gratitude. They insist that they have little for which to be grateful. There can be times in our lives when we seem to have nothing. Friends, counselors, or spiritual leaders may encourage us to give thanks for the gift of life, but what of those people who want to end their lives? For what will they be grateful? Let us take note that I Thessalonians 5:18 does not tell us to be thankful *for* all circumstances, but *in* all circumstances. This, we will discover, is sound advice.

Happy people are thankful people. Casual observers say that they are happy because of the state of their lives. In nearly every example of truly happy people, we will find that there was a time when the circumstances of their lives were quite different from what we currently see. What touches us about these people is that their thanksgiving does not need an object. There doesn't have to be any outer thing to be thankful about. For truly happy people, thanksgiving is a choice, and the same insight can be helpful for people who are unhappy. Even the person with only the proverbial "shirt on his back" has the capacity to choose to be grateful.

Enter his gates with thanksgiving and his courts with praise! This is an ancient belief expressed in Psalm 100:4. Long ago, seekers in search of God found that thankfulness was a doorway to God's presence. The ancients envisioned God as a walled city, difficult to enter. Through hymns of praise and a basic and essential attitude of gratitude, they found themselves in God's presence. They literally experienced their Creator.

This became their experience not because God needed their thanks or praise. God is not so small as to need anything from us. In fact, there is nothing that these ancient seekers did or we can do today that can change God. The truth is that thanksgiving changes us. Thankfulness actually becomes an avenue for God's power. This is why Jesus expressed thanksgiving before He performed what we call miracles. For instance, before five thousand were fed from five loaves of bread and two fish, Jesus gave thanks for what He had. Likewise, as Jesus stood before the tomb of Lazarus, He gave thanks before He called him to rise from the dead. This form of gratitude is an act of faith because it comes before the fact, before anything happens.

Give Thanks in All Circumstances

Paul and Silas also experienced the wonder of thanksgiving as they shared a prison cell. As the Scripture reveals in Acts 16:25-26, around midnight the two men were singing and praising God. Their circumstances did not warrant thanksgiving, but they made a conscious choice to praise God. Their uplifted consciousness became an avenue for God's power, and the power of an earthquake opened their prison cell. Their souls were free through thankfulness, and therefore their freedom became manifest in the outer world.

This is the way we are called to live. We are not to give thanks for circumstances; we are to give thanks while in the midst of all circumstances. There is no time when thanksgiving will not open a doorway to God's presence and power.

It is not that our actions coerce God into action. In truth, all the potential love, wisdom, strength, power, and peace are always available to us. We live and move and have our being in a sea of all-sufficiency. What is needed is a window or doorway through which it can flow into our lives. Just as every candle needs a wick before the wax of the candle can give forth its light, so, too, does Spirit need an avenue for Its expression. It is not that thanksgiving opens the door; thanksgiving is the door. As we live lives of thankfulness,

Spirit has the wick It needs. All the potential power of God becomes real to us and flows into our lives and the world.

Through thanksgiving, we rise above circumstances. Gratitude is like a lifting wind, but it does more than lift us above conditions. First, it takes us from an earthly state of consciousness that is rooted in the limitations of human thought to a state of mind and heart in which the seemingly unattainable is possible.

The process is a simple one, but consistent in its effect. We find ourselves in a difficult situation. We can look for something to be thankful about, and we may find it. I remember a story about Joe, a young man in the midst of his ministerial training. It was a time to bond with the other students and express the love of God that they studied each day. The problem was that there was one student that Joe could hardly endure. He went to a spiritual advisor and asked for help. She told him to look at the student minister he disliked and find something about the man he could genuinely praise. After a time, Joe returned to say that there was nothing about the man that he liked. She told him to look again, and he finally saw something he liked: the man's tie. He told his counselor about this breakthrough, and she told Joe to tell the man that he liked his tie. He did so, and immediately the other student took off the tie and gave it to Joe. A door opened, and they became best friends.

Give Thanks in All Circumstances

This is one illustration of the power of genuine gratitude. Thanksgiving is the door, but there may be times when there is nothing we see for which we are thankful. Joe was close to such an experience. Perhaps some people would tell us that there is always something for which we can give thanks. Obviously, this can be done, but remember what the ancients discovered: We can simply choose to be thankful. As we begin to utter words of gratitude, we are lifted up. The door begins to form.

We always have the ability to give thanks. We can chant the words, "Thank you, God." We can think again and again, "Thank you, dear Friend", and we can do this in all circumstances. In this way, we are not limited by situations. The conditions of our lives don't have to be a certain way before we can be happy. We can choose to be thankful in all circumstances. This is the will of God. We have been given this capacity, and when it is joined to prayer and joy, life is as it is meant to be.

FORTY-DAY GUIDE TO ATTAINING THE UNATTAINABLE

God's Will in Action

Reading *Attaining the Unattainable, The Will of God* may be enough for you. You may feel that you can establish your own way of integrating the ideas in the book into your life, or perhaps you are feeling that you have only just begun. You want more. You are willing to at least try to know God, rejoice always, pray constantly, and give thanks in all circumstances. You are willing to attempt the seemingly impossible, but you need help.

The Forty-Day Guide was written for you. It will take you through the book again and ask you some personal questions to help you understand the steps *you* need to take. What you will find is that it is more than just a summary of the ideas in this book. The Guide will challenge you to live with new purpose and direction. It is filled with exercises and additional insights whose purpose is to put the principles in the book to the test. This is the way it is with spiritual things—they are never done and put on the shelf. If they are worth their salt, they become a part of our lives. They are like the food and drink that becomes our bodies. They become the foundation of our lives.

Why forty days? First, forty is a symbolic number. In the Bible, the number forty appears again and again. It rained forty days and forty nights, and the

ATTAINING THE UNATTAINABLE

God's Will in Action

earth was flooded. The Hebrews wandered in the wilderness forty years, and Jesus was tempted after fasting forty days. The number forty is not a coincidence. It represents the time required to complete a task.

I believe it will take you more than forty literal days to complete the guide portion of the book because you will find from time to time that you want to spend more than one day on an exercise or that you'll want to give attention to a previous day's lesson to glean more insight into the ideas you previously explored. You can go from day to day, but it is best to pause when you feel the need and rest with the ideas and practices that challenge and enliven you.

You will write in the guide, and years later you will return to reread what you have written, and the words will tell you the story of your growth. You will also discover that you are a different person than you were in previous years, and therefore you will answer the questions differently than before.

The Forty-Day Guide will not only take you through the book again, but it will take you deeper into your inner self and provide support as you attempt to attain the unattainable.

"The only way to discover the limits of the possible is to go beyond them into the impossible."
ARTHUR C. CLARKE, Inventor and Novelist

"There are those who look at things the way they are, and ask why…
I dream of things that never were, and ask why not?"
ROBERT FRANCIS KENNEDY

DAY **1** | My Perception of God's Will is Unlimited

Over the course of my life I have heard many opinions about the will of God. Some people make God's will complex and therefore more than it really is. Other people make it less than its true self. For example, they may think of God's will as a particular action when in truth it is a way of life. In this instance, they underestimated the unlimited reach of God's will.

What are some opinions you have heard about the will of God?

Indicate some of your past beliefs concerning God's will.

DAY **2** | **I Have a Personal Will**

I admit, I have a personal will. Often I expect things the way I want them. Here is my cry, "Not your will, but mine be done." In this instance, "your will" could be God's, but it could also be another person's.

Give an example of a time when you asserted your personal will.

How did you assert your will? How did you try to get your way? There are numerous techniques that you are well aware of, but there are some that you don't realize at the time. For example, you might use logic or guilt, you might try to bribe others to do something, you may cry large crocodile tears for sympathy, or you may even use anger to try and intimidate others. What technique works for you?

DAY **3** | **Today My Beginning is Willingness**

Remember that your will is a not a negative thing. If you did not have a faculty of will, there is little you would accomplish. In fact, the great challenges of life are first met with willingness. You may not know the first tangible step to take, but you can begin, for the beginning is willingness.

Think of something that has been a challenge for you, something that you have not yet accomplished, then let willingness be your beginning. Write a statement that expresses your willingness to face this challenge or accomplish this deed.

DAY **4** | I Am Willingness

Change often begins with a word. You state what you want to accomplish or what you are willing to begin. The origin of the statement begins as a thought, it impacts your mind, then becomes a part of your consciousness.

This practice has helped me for many years. It works, but it is only the beginning. Sweeping, far-reaching, and unpredictable transformation happens when you identify with what you desire. It becomes part of you.

There is a story about a meditation student who was told by a master to enter into a small room and meditate on a bull. The student was in the room for three days. After this time, the master called for him to come out. The student replied, "My horns won't fit through the door." He identified with his object of meditation.

Let us identify with willingness. You do this by using an identity phrase—I am. Whenever you use these two words, you identify with something. You begin a journey toward becoming the object of the *I am*. For instance, you might give attention to the following idea: *I am love*.

Today, let us give attention to the statement of the day—*I am willingness*. As you identify with willingness, what effect does this practice have on your life?

DAY **5** | # Willingness is a Call for Energy and Power

Today is a day of feeling. You are most likely sensing the fruit of willingness—energy and power. When you assert your personal will, you may feel powerful, but the power is self-contained. It is in your human self, and therefore, is easily depleted. Willingness opens you to infinite power and energy.

When you assert your personal will, you usually think you know exactly what must happen. When you are willing, you open yourself to unseen possibilities. This is how life becomes extraordinary. You don't know what is best, but energy and power that transcends you sweeps you along like a twig in a river. You don't know where it is taking you, but because its origin is divine, you know it is for a greater good than you could ever imagine.

Can you feel the power today? Are you willing to let it take you where it will? If you answer yes to these questions, you are one day closer to attaining the unattainable.

Describe your emotions as they relate to your energy and power.

DAY **6** | **Today, I Surrender My Personal Will**

Feeling the power of willingness, you are now prepared to begin to surrender your personal will. Begin with the statement above. Think the thought and pause on each word. Are there any words to which you react negatively? If you do, this is most likely your weaker-self resisting the relinquishing of its will. Like King Herod who resisted the birth of Jesus, your personal will is uncomfortable with the birth of willingness in your soul.

After you mentally explore the statement above, speak audibly today's affirmation: "Today, I surrender my personal will." Say it again and again, a total of seven times. Pause each time you speak and sense your reaction to the words. Don't hurry. Speak and feel.

In the space below write today's statement seven times. This is an ideal process. You begin with thought, move to the spoken word, and then put the words into motion and make them more authentic by seeing them emerge from your pen or pencil.

DAY 7 | Not My Will, but God's be Done

You may have a personal will, but there is a wisdom that far exceeds the human mind. Will and understanding are soulmates on the spiritual journey. We have our personal desires, but we cannot fathom the full effects of our actions.

In the Garden of Gethsemane, Jesus asked if it was possible for the cup He saw before Him to be cast aside. This was His personal will, His human desire, but He knew firsthand the greater wisdom that ruled His life and the universe. His response is one you can adopt, "Not my will, but yours be done" (Lk. 42:22). These seven words convey powerful ideas. They say, "I don't know what is best." The seven words acknowledge the unknown and mysterious aspects of life. We tend to think if we know what lies ahead, we are safe and secure, but there is no security without faith.

Is the great unknown before you? Rest assured that if you answered "no," you spoke only a half-truth, for mystery and the unknown are always nearby. Here is my question to you: Is there any day of your life when it is inappropriate to say to your Creator, "Not my will, but Yours will be done"?

List some examples of how this can help your life.

DAY 8 | God's Will is not a Happening; It is not an Event

Today's statement is one of the most important ideas in *Attaining The Unattainable, The Will of God* for it challenges thousands of years of preconceived thought and belief about the divine will. However, once you recover from the shock of the challenge, this single insight will open you to new possibilities. It naturally causes you to search for another understanding of divine will. If the will of God is not an event or happening, what is it?

List events you thought (hoped) were God's will.

Are you willing to declare that these events were not God's will?

DAY 9 | "Know Me"

With today's lesson, we begin to explore a new understanding of the will of God. This is the beginning of a new way of life, a life in which we live from a divine center.

God's will is "know Me." In other words, we are being perpetually called to know and experience our Creator. Once we experience the Presence, a new consciousness dawns in us, and the good news is that all states of consciousness or awareness manifest themselves in and as our lives.

Consider the joy and gratitude you will know when your consciousness of God dawns in your life. The two words, "know Me," reveal your purpose. Through the experience of the Presence, you are blessed, but it is also through your consciousness that Spirit has an avenue through which to manifest Itself in the world.

Today, there is no specific exercise or spiritual practice. Instead, simply ponder these things in your heart, for they hold great promise for the life you are destined and deserve to live.

DAY 10 | I Am Willing to Know God as Wisdom

It is possible to let the words "know Me" be the center of everything you do. When you have a challenge, the answer is to know and experience the Presence. When life runs smoothly, the momentum is maintained when you continue to give attention to Spirit and to spiritual things.

There is practicality in knowing God. Here is an example. Consider the situation in which you have an important decision to make. Many people would ask if it is God's will that you decide one specific way, or is it God's will that you make another choice. The answer is neither. God's will is that you know Him.

And here is where the practicality comes to bear in your life. When you know God as wisdom or experience Spirit as wisdom or light, decisions are made. Actually, the choice simply comes from within us, and we know what to do.

The next time you have a choice to make, let go of the decision and its supposed importance. Instead, give attention to God as wisdom and allow this awareness to be born in you. Rest assured that from this new consciousness, light will shine, and you will know what to do.

When your time comes to let the light shine (make a decision), return to this day and describe your process in the space below.

DAY 11 | I Am Willing to Know God as Life

Maintaining a balanced life can be a challenge that confronts you with many decisions. From time to time, illness may cause concern when it affects you or a family member or friend. In the past, you may have wondered if it is God's will that you or another be healed, but now you know God's will is neither health or sickness. God's will is "know Me." In truth, the illness has placed before you the possibility of knowing God as life and wholeness. Often the manifestation of this consciousness is a healed body or mind.

When the body is ill, I think and talk positively and constructively about my body, but I don't allow it to dominate my attention. Instead, I intensify my focus on God's will and answer the call to know and reconnect with the Great Physician who created me. I open myself to experience God as life, for in this life I know there is no disease or discomfort. Through grace, as I know God as life, I am healed.

The great difficulty for most is to keep the mind focused on God when you are in discomfort or pain. This is when it is a good idea to ask for prayer help from a prayerful individual who has heard the call as you have to know the Great Physician.

During the time of your next healing challenge or the healing challenge of someone close to you, return to this day and write about what unfolded from within you and in your life as you became increasingly willing to know God as life.

DAY **12** | **I Am Willing to Know**
God as My Source

Any difficulty of human life can be met by responding to God's will, "know Me." Many a person has prospered during a time of seeming lack by experiencing God as the source.

Once again, the challenge is to take your eyes off the need and focus on the source of all. You would think this would be easy to do, but the mind has been trained to seek security in the world, and so that is where it looks. It is time for you to take command and determine where you will place your attention. There is good advice in the Scripture, "I lift up my eyes to the hills. From whence does my help come? My help comes from the Lord…" (Ps. 121:1-2). This is another expression of God's will.

Dear friend, as you know God as your source, you will prosper. Lack will lose its power over you, and you will know peace, security, and well-being. Remember, it is not God's will that you prosper in any specific way, but that you know God as your source. Then this consciousness will manifest itself as your life, and all will be well.

As you apply these principles to your next prosperity challenge, return to this day and record the experience in the space provided below.

DAY **13** | **The Answer to Every Challenge is to Know God**

If you let God's call, "know Me," be the center of your life, you will enter into the mystical dimension of life. You will put to the test Jesus' statement, "...seek first the kingdom...and all these things shall be added unto you" (Mt. 6:33).

Long ago I saw the possibilities of this way of life. It made sense to me. I ought to be able to give attention to spiritual things and have my earthly life flow forth from my relationship with the Presence. Essentially, I put Jesus' statement to the test. As you can imagine, He was correct. There is no challenge of soul, mind, body, or worldly condition that cannot be met by knowing God. And there is more. As you seek the kingdom, your spiritual life will deepen, and you will experience firsthand the reality of things unseen.

In the coming week, put Jesus' statement to the test by knowing God. There may be some problem to solve, but more importantly, simply give attention to Spirit and see what happens. Become sensitive not so much to outer changes as to your beliefs about yourself, others, life, and God. Take note of your feelings and thoughts and developing attitudes.

In the space below write about your experience and, in particular, your thoughts, feelings, and beliefs.

DAY **14** It is My Purpose to be in the Presence of the King

Imagine that you are a minister of state for a mighty king. What is your daily task? Do you come before the monarch each day, bow, and ask, "O Mighty One, what is your will for me today?" The answer is, "No." The work of a minister of state is not to ask the king what to do; your work is to be in the presence of the King. Then when the king wants something done, he needs only to call on you and assign you your task.

Can you see how this illustration can guide you in your relationship with Spirit? You are not to continuously ask what you should do. Your work is to be in the presence of the Creator. Of course, you are in the presence of God because you live and move and have your being in God's presence, but the call of Day Fourteen is to be consciously aware that you live in God.

Whenever you are consciously aware of God, you are potentially an instrument of the activity of God. The "King" can speak to you and guide your actions and your life. So your work is not to ask God what to do; your work is to be consciously in the presence of God.

What steps will you take to support the purpose of being in the presence of the King?

_____

_____

_____

Here is a prayer and meditation practice you may find helpful. In your quiet time today, imagine yourself to be in the court of a mighty king. Look around you at the surroundings and the people who are present. Observe the workings of the court. Take note of what you are wearing and where you are seated, and remember that your purpose is to be in the presence of the king.

_____

_____

_____

_____

DAY 15 | God's Will is a Way of Life

There is a perspective that declares God's will is one thing for one person and something different for another person. This is not your way of life. In your approach to life, God's will is the same for everyone. Everyone has the same destiny—closeness with the Creator that eventually becomes what it is—oneness.

You are engineered to know God. This is not the destiny of a blessed few. It is the life each of us is to live. The question is, are you willing to let go of the belief that God's will is one thing for one person and something else for another person? Are you willing to believe God's will is the same for everyone and that the divine will is a way of life?

What is your answer to these questions about God's will?

DAY **16** God Wants Only the Best for You

When you read or hear the statement for today, what thought comes to mind? Do you think of a loving relationship, a prosperous job, peace of mind, or material things? Often people will say that God wants them to drive an expensive car. Not really...People tend to think that the statement, "God wants only the best for you," refers to earthly conditions. The truth is that the best that God wants for you is not earthly. It is the pearl of great price for which you will sell everything in order to obtain it.

It is the age-old question: do you want the harvest of the apple orchard today, or do you want the orchard for years to come? Remember, God's will for us is not material; God's will is spiritual. The pearl of great price Jesus spoke of in Mt. 13:45-46 was not a tangible pearl. He spoke of something more valuable than any earthly thing. This pearl of great price is a consciousness of God.

This is what God is offering you. The truth is Spirit is offering you Itself and from this gift will come all the blessings of life. God does want only the best for you, and the best you could ever receive is an experience of the Presence.

DAY 17 | The Will of God is a Call to Action

Many people think of God's will in terms of the things that God does. For this person, God's will includes God's actions. You are discovering another insight into God's will. God's will is a call for action—yours. God is calling for you to act, to live life in a certain way.

In the space below, indicate what you feel yourself being called to do. In other words, what is God's will for you?

DAY 18 | God's Will is a Life of Joy

Have you ever said that what you truly want for your children is that they be happy? Nearly every parent makes this declaration. The parent may have some specifics in mind, but happiness is the common denominator.

God's will for you is similar. The divine will is that you live a life of joy. If this is true, it must be that the forces of the universe are poised to assist you as you live this life.

Today, say the following statement to yourself again and again— "joy is natural."

DAY **19** | I Return Again and Again to Joy

Joy may be natural, but it is most likely not always your experience. You find joy only to lose it again. It is because of this aspect of the human journey that Spirit says to us, "Rejoice always."

No matter what happens to you that seems to cause your joy to dissolve, you are to return again and again to the truth that God's will for you is a life of joy. Your destiny is joy. Today is a reminder of this truth.

Today and in the coming days, take note of your thoughts and words to determine if they support or oppose the statement that joy is your destiny. For instance, do you find yourself saying or thinking that you have bad luck or that things never go smoothly for you? Such thoughts oppose the natural force of the universe that calls you to joy.

When you realize your thinking is contrary to God's will, say no to your thoughts and declare that no matter how many times your joy seems to escape, you refuse to believe anything less than joy is God's will for you.

DAY **20** | I Refuse to Accept Anything Less than Joy

It is time to take a stand! You are never to settle for anything less than joy. Do you know anyone who has given up on joy and happiness? This person has experienced great difficulties and come to believe that the difficulties are normal. It is also most likely that he or she has also experienced joy, but has chosen to focus on the problems of life and the negative emotions or circumstances.

Basically, a choice was made. The person settled for something less than joy. Not you! You refuse to accept anything less than joy for your life.

Here's a suggestion: send an email to me at roseij@embarqmail.com and tell me that you have joined the thousands of other people who have refused to settle for anything less than joy. Make it a quick note. Do it now. I look forward to hearing from you.

DAY **21** | My Joy is not Born of Circumstance

Today, you begin to "define" your joy in a new way. Most people's happiness or joy depends upon certain things happening. When they don't happen, there is no joy. If your joy is dependent upon conditions, your joy will rise and fall. When it falls, you can always rejoice again and remind yourself that God's will for you is joy. The next logical step is to acknowledge that, in the past, your joy was condition-dependent.

Only by acknowledging this belief can a joy be born in you that does not depend upon outer circumstances.

In the space below, write seven examples of times when you lost your sense of joy because it depended upon something happening.

DAY **22** I Feel God's Pleasure

True joy comes from within. This joy is dependent upon something, but not upon earthly circumstances or the words or actions of others. The joy that is your destiny is rooted in God and the statement, "I feel God's pleasure." Could you imagine a greater joy?

Here is a great truth. Whenever a person experiences God's presence, Spirit has an avenue through which to express Itself. This expression can take many forms, but often the person will discover a hidden talent or suddenly feel compelled to begin a new endeavor. And this is the astounding thing...as the talent is expressed or steps are taken to "do a new thing," the individual experiences joy.

Is there anything in your life today where you experience great joy, where it is obvious that something greater than yourself is flowing through you? If there is, rejoice and give thanks. If such an experience is currently not a part of your life, fear not, for the many ideas and practices in this book will help you come to the time when you will experience the Presence. Then as Spirit pours Itself through your soul, you will feel God's pleasure.

DAY **23** | **Giving is Pure Joy**

Today's spiritual practice is a simple one guaranteed to bring joy and cause you to ask why you didn't do this long ago. Dear friend, put to the test today's affirmation: "Giving is pure joy."

Do this by planning to give an anonymous gift to someone. He or she must never know it came from you. Even before you give the gift or put it in the mail, you will begin to experience this form of pure joy. Just thinking about whom you will give the gift to will open you to joy. Selecting the gift will add to your joy, and then when you give the gift, joy will flood your being, for giving is pure joy. Put it to the test.

DAY **24** | # When I Lose Myself, I Experience Pure Joy

Joy rests not in you, but in the fullness and wholeness of creation. As long as you maintain your identity as separate from the whole, joy will elude you. However, when you lose yourself, joy will join you.

Here is the question. What are you doing when you lose yourself? For some people it is prayer, and you will be exploring prayer and meditation in the coming days, but there are other ways you lose yourself. You can paint, read, play a sport, volunteer, etc.

One of the ways I lose myself is writing. As I write to you now, I wish I had kept track of the many times I lost myself and experienced joy as I wrote *Attaining The Unattainable, The Will of God*. You, too, can have the experience of pure joy if you lose yourself.

Return to this page in the future and record a time when you lost yourself, touched the wholeness of creation, and experienced pure joy.

DAY 25 | Prayer is God's Will

The statement is obvious—God's will is a call to action. It is a call to pray. Notice that there is no directive as to how to pray; you are simply to pray.

It is my belief that a diligent commitment to prayer will cause your prayer life to change, grow, and evolve. As you pray, you will have experiences that will challenge and guide you. Your prayers may initially be about the world, but this, too, will change. The most important insight of this day is that it is God's will that you pray, for if you do, not only will your prayer life change, you will change as well. Today, remember this one thing—prayer is God's will.

DAY **26** | **Prayer is Not of this World**

It may take years, but eventually you will conclude that prayer is not of this world. Consider that if prayer is God's will, and God transcends earthly things, prayer must transcend worldly concerns as well.

For today, it is not necessary to know what prayer is, but only what it is not. Prayer is not of this world. Reflect upon this idea.

If the statement "Prayer is not of this world" is new and challenging to you, pretend that it is true for twenty-four hours, and record below any insights that come to you.

DAY 27 | God's Will is Oneness

When you consider yesterday's idea that prayer is not of this world, numerous insights can come to you. Many years ago, reflecting upon the idea that prayer is not of this world led me to the idea that prayer's purpose is oneness. It is through prayer that we discover and experience our oneness with God and all creation.

Through the ages, most likely before the age of remembering, human beings experienced oneness with creation and with something greater than self. Once this occurred, it was normal to not only want to re-experience the oneness, but to live from it. For those people who have seen the oneness of all life, it is a natural step to believe that God's will is oneness.

It may seem as if true oneness is seldom experienced, but the truth is that it is not extraordinary, it is *extra* ordinary. It is your destiny. It is the life you are to live.

This is a powerful extension of the call to pray constantly. If prayer is oneness with God, it is to be your constant experience. You are to live in oneness. It is God's will.

DAY 28 | I Am One with God and All Creation

Today, step into the fullness of God's will by declaring with your words and actions, "I am one with God and all creation." At least once each waking hour, speak these words audibly. This is a challenge, but the practice will help you remember that you are to live a life of oneness. However, the real challenge is to declare your oneness with God and all creation through your actions by the way you live your life. This is your challenge, not solely to speak, but to act.

Don't dismiss today's call to action. It can take months before the truth of the words you speak become rooted in your soul, but actions reinforce ideas quickly and establish the foundation of your life.

In the space below, list some of your own actions that declared your oneness with God and all creation.

DAY **29** | Prayer is Oneness

Through the years, my ideas about prayer have changed drastically. Today, I feel prayer is an experience of God's presence. What I once called prayer I now call my prayer practices which are many and varied. I may speak affirmations, contemplate the flame of a candle, count my breath, reflect on a word, or simply sit in silence, none of which are considered an "act" of prayer. They are my prayer practices.

Prayer is oneness. It is an experience, and the greatest experience is the realization that you are a part of everything, and everything is a part of you. Prayer practices support this approach to life, but they are not the experience. They help to prepare you for the life you are destined to live, the life that is God's will—a life of oneness.

Explain how your perception of prayer has changed from your childhood, through the significant stages of your life, to the present.

DAY **30** | I Practice the Presence of God

If the will of God is prayer and if the divine will is oneness, then it is time for you to give attention to the practice of the presence of God. Brother Lawrence, a Carmelite monk of the 17th century, worked in the kitchen of his monastery. At first, he hated it, but then he made a decision. He would wed everything he did to the contemplation of God. His experience of the Presence became so powerful that he said he experienced joys so great that he could hardly contain them. This is what happens when a person prays constantly. There is little formal prayer. In its place is the realization of the presence of God.

It is this way of life you are to begin today. Most likely there will be many beginnings as you practice the Presence. For a time you will remember God, but there will also be times when you forget that God even exists. God is with you in all your tasks during one day, and the next day, you hardly give God a thought.

There are numerous practices for this way of life. You will undoubtedly discover your own, but here are a few ideas:

1. When you bathe, think of the water as God's presence cleansing you.
2. When you eat, bring to mind the manna in the desert and how the birds fed the prophet.
3. When you have a task before you, say to yourself, "I of myself can do nothing, through Christ I can do all things."
4. Give every person you meet a silent greeting, "The presence of God in me beholds the presence of God in you."
5. Pause from time to time and look around you and imagine that God is playing a game of hide and seek with you until you feel God close at hand.
6. Before you sleep at night, ask that you be divinely guided and illumined in your dreams.

These are but a few ideas to help you practice the Presence. Put them to the test and see if you, too, experience a joy so great that you can barely contain it.

DAY **31** | I See God Everywhere

Yesterday, you began the practice of the presence of God. It is destined to be a life-long pursuit that will result in the realization that God is everywhere and in everyone. Let today be a day of quiet observation. Consciously look for God in all things and all people. To see what has always been and always shall be, you must be lifted up in consciousness to a new vision. God is here. God is there. God is everywhere.

People have described this breakthrough as a sheer veil falling from their eyes. You may not have this sensation, but you will most likely say as did Jacob, "How awesome is this place and I knew it not."

DAY **32** | # A Thought of Separation is a Call to Prayer

There is a great oneness that exists between all things, but as you know, there are times when you do not feel this oneness—you have a sense of separation. Often there is a feeling of fear with thoughts of separation. Rather than believing yourself to be a part of everything, you feel apart from everything.

When these times come, please remember that a thought of separation is a call to prayer, a call to oneness. In this way, the thought or feeling of separation becomes a part of your spiritual practice. It asks you to pray and remember that you are a part of everyone and everything.

DAY **33** | **Today, I Learn the Prayer of the Heart**

The prayer of the heart is an ancient tradition and spiritual practice. It is worthy of your attention. You might want to read the book, *The Way of the Pilgrim*, for it tells the tale of a Russian pilgrim whose life's center was the prayer of the heart.

When you pray this prayer, you link your breath and eventually your heartbeat to a verbal prayer. The words used by the Russian pilgrim may be words that are not a part of your spiritual tradition. If that is the case, use words that are meaningful to you. The pilgrim's prayer was "Lord Jesus, have mercy on me for I am a sinner." I have used the following statement when I prayed the prayer of the heart, "My God, my all, I love you." (I have always liked seven syllable phrases because they have a rhythm to them in the same way that your breathing and heartbeat are rhythmic.)

Today, select the phrase that you will use as the prayer of the heart and write it below.

Link the prayer to your breathing and hold in mind some of the words as you inhale and the remaining words as you exhale. Eventually, you will want to center your attention on your heart as you pray. The result will be that breath, words, heartbeat, and therefore your life will all be linked in the circle that is God's presence.

DAY **34** | God is a Part of Everything I Do

Notice that over the course of the last few days, your life and prayer are now one. The practices you have learned are not rituals; they are attempts to join the consciousness of God and your daily life. This, I am convinced, is God's will. God is a part of everything you do.

Surely, this is what is meant by *pray constantly*. Live life knowing that God is always with you as you live in oneness with the One.

Write any comments you have about this aspect of God's will.

DAY 35 | God's Will is Thankfulness

It is stated clearly...through God's will, you give thanks in all circumstances. What a challenge this can be as you see the divine pattern emerge. You are to live a life of joy. You are to live a life of conscious oneness with God and all creation, and you are to live a life of thankfulness.

Today, it is not necessary to know how to live this life, but to open yourself to the possibility of a life of gratitude. This is our old friend *willingness* at work in your life. You are willing to live a life of thankfulness. "How?" is not today's question. The question is...are you willing?

DAY 36 — I Give Thanks for the Blessings of My Life

Yesterday, you acknowledged that thanksgiving is a vital part of God's will. Today, you begin to live your life accordingly. To begin, give thanks for the blessings of your life.

In the past, I have asked people to make a list of 100 things for which they are thankful. Who could make such a list? At first, you might think that 100 items is too many. The reason I suggest a list of 100 items is to loosen the mind, so thanksgiving can flow like the mighty river it is. Soon the people making the list are giving thanks for the birds that fly and the sun on their face on an autumn day, and stillness of the air early in the evening. One thought of thankfulness attracts another.

Dear friend, as you give thanks for the many blessings of your life, you will find there is so much more to be thankful for. Such is the power of gratitude.

In the space below, get started on your list of blessings. It is not necessary to make the list of 100, but list your blessings until you feel a lightness in your soul and the anticipation of a greater good to come.

DAY 37 | I Give Thanks for the Challenges of My Life

It is one thing to give thanks for your blessings; it is quite another thing to give thanks for the challenges of your life. This is your task today. It will eventually lead to a way of life that is in concert with God's will, for it is the divine will that you give thanks in *all* circumstances.

By taking this step, you open yourself to the greater good just as you did by making a list of your blessings. Usually, when a person considers giving thanks for the challenges of life, the hardship of the challenges tend to distract their attention away from the many blessings they still have so they wonder what there is to give thanks for. This is the question we are to ask. This question is the beginning of the growth that accompanies any life challenge. Giving thanks in *all* circumstances is the beginning of a spiritual breakthrough.

In the space below, give thanks for the challenges of your life. You might want to take the following approach. Write a statement such as, "I give thanks for (insert the challenge), for it is calling me to a life I have never lived before."

DAY **38** | I Choose Gratitude

By giving thanks for the blessings and the challenging circumstances of your life, you will discover that thanksgiving is an avenue for God's expression. Once this realization takes root in you, you will see a new way to live.

You will simply choose gratitude and thanksgiving. The truth is that you don't need something for which to be thankful. You can be thankful . . . period. You know what it is to express gratitude for blessings and challenges. You know the feeling associated with gratitude, so you can take the next step into the kingdom of God. You can choose to be grateful. Make that choice now!

DAY **39** | ## Thanksgiving is the Door to God's Presence

When you choose gratitude, you discover that thanksgiving is a door or gateway to God's presence. This is the message of Psalm 100, "Enter into (God's) gates with praise and thanksgiving."

Thankfulness awakens the mind to the miracles of life, but the greatest blessing of all is that a thankful person knows God. When you choose gratitude, you choose God. Another earthly blessing doesn't have to manifest itself. Another challenge doesn't have to be met. You walk through the door of thanksgiving and find yourself in God's presence. This consciousness of the One is life's greatest blessing.

Can you see that this is true? Is it your experience that this is true? If not, how else will you discover that thanksgiving is the door to God's Presence?

DAY **40** | God's Will is Life

Knowing God's will is your life, a life of joy; you are to rejoice always. God's will is a life of oneness, for you are to pray without ceasing. God's will is a life of thanksgiving, for you are to give thanks in all circumstances.

You can now see that God's will is calling you to action. You can now see that the divine will is not circumstance or happenings. God's will is not expressed as events, but as the life you live. It is now for you to go forth and live this life. And please, know that you are not alone. Thousands of people are also striving to attain the unattainable. It may seem difficult, but the energy of the universe is leading you and all who share this way of life.

Know Me!

Rejoice always, pray constantly, and give thanks in all circumstances... for this is the will of God...

I Thessalonians 5:16-18

There are few subjects more puzzling than God's will. What is it? It seems so complex. Every generation wrestles with the question of whether one thing is God's will or another. One thing is certain: Humanity believes that there is a divine intent. This is just as indisputable as the fact that there is personal will. I believe the reason our understanding of God's will is so convoluted and mysterious is that we persist in thinking of it in terms of our earthly lives. In our minds, events and God's will are entwined with one another. As long as this kind of thought endures, we will be puzzled by the condition of our lives. We will wonder if a disaster is the will of God. Some will say yes, and others will say no. The debate will continue, and we will be no closer to knowing the divine intent.

Know Me!

It is my hope that *Attaining the Unattainable, The Will of God* has helped you to see divine intent differently. It is found not in happenings and human conditions, but as a way of life. God's will is *Know Me*. This insight becomes a way of life. We can see that we are to experience God as life, and then we can be healed. As we know God as wisdom, we are wise and creative. This simple insight and two simple words, "Know Me," changed my life, and they can change yours as well.

Through the pages of this book, we have discovered that God's will is a life of joy, oneness with all creation, and thankfulness. Knowing this does not make the task any easier. In fact, when we receive the challenge to rejoice always, pray constantly, and give thanks in all circumstances, this way of life appears beyond our reach—unattainable.

The great difficulty with the seemingly impossible is that we tend to not even try; however, it is the impossible things that have the greatest potential. They require the greatest courage and cause the most enduring and far-reaching change. When we attempt the impossible, we must discover our hidden gifts and abilities. How else can we do the impossible?

Let us welcome the challenge of the unattainable. If I can experience for a brief time the kind of life I am told I can live, I will have a star to follow. Perhaps

I don't have to fully conform to all aspect of God's will all at once. I don't have to rejoice always, pray constantly, give thanks in all circumstances, and seek to know Him all at once. Maybe I can begin with one. Might the one lead me to the others? Could it be that joy, oneness, thanksgiving, and knowing God are all entwined with one another?

I remember that for years the driving force and core of my life was Know Me. It still is, but, in a way unknown to me, these two words and their implications have led me to God's will for me: joy, oneness, and thanksgiving. It is as if I began a quest not for a chalice from which Jesus drank, but for a way of life He lived thousands of years ago. May it be that my journey is not a solitary one. Please join me in the way of life that is God's will, a way of life that is our destiny.

If the message of this book is in tune
with your approach to living, please write to

Jim and Nancy Rosemergy
PO Box 7314
Ft Myers FL 33911

to receive a free copy
of the *Inner Journey Journey*
and *Inner Journey Letter*, as well as
additional information about a life of
oneness with God.